Cataclysm

Katarina Rivers

BookLeaf Publishing
India | USA | UK

Made with ❤ on the BookLeaf Publishing Platform
www.bookleafpub.in
www.bookleafpub.com

Dedication

To all those who have been forged by fire.

Preface

Cataclysm:

-a large-scale and violent event in the natural world.

-a sudden violent upheaval, especially in a political or social context.

Acknowledgements

This third book would not have been possible without the continued love and support of so many people who are incredibly precious to me. Your love has fueled my healing, your encouragement has opened so many doors for me, and your compassion has shown me that even after chaos there will (eventually) be clarity.

1. An Act of Resistance

Learning to love myself,
Not for what I can do,
But simply for who I am
Has been the most radical protest
I've ever participated in.
It has been the longest journey
And it is still going.

2. All Eyes

I cannot write
About happiness,
About the beauty and joy of the world
When I have witnessed the terror of it.
I have seen parents dragging their children's lifeless bodies
Out of the ruins of what used to be their safety-
Their homes,
Their schools and playgrounds,
Their hospitals,
The hallowed halls of worship,
Refugee camps they fled to
In a desperate attempt to protect their children
I looked on as a father held his daughter,
Her eyes closed, skin pale and cold,
I heard his tearful begging for her to come back
Or for Allah to take him with her.
His daughter, so small and fragile in his strong arms-
Arms that could never have stopped bombs,
Although he would have tried I have no doubt.

I can hear the swan song in my mind,
The wails of a broken man ringing in my ears.
I have seen the very moment
A person's soul is eviscerated
But their lungs continue to expand,
Their heart continues to beat,
A physical betrayal to the emotional turmoil churning inside.
So how can I highlight
All of the 'good' in this world when
I close my eyes
And all that I can see is the cruelty and depravity of man?
I cannot write a pretty poem
To placate you
While a genocide is happening oceans away
And my government not only turns a blind eye
But also funds it,
Basking in their complicitness,
Feigning concern while embracing the spoils of war.
How can I profess the miracles of life
When I have seen the bodies?

3. Conviction

Many talk
In a crowded
Congregation.
Many claim
To be of God,
Of the church.
But so few
Listen to their own
Teachings,
Even fewer obey.
Hypocrisy can never be
Righteous.

4. Alyona

The night you died
Is forever imprinted in my very soul.
I slept on an air mattress in your living room
With your son in his playpen beside me,
Just within arm's reach.

Your husband had always been a heavy sleeper,
So you had always been the one up at night with all of the babies.
And then suddenly, without warning,
You were gone.
So I stayed beside your son,
Who looked so very much like you.

He woke up nearly every hour that first night-
Crying out.
We all thought at first maybe he was hungry
Or perhaps his stomach was having difficulty
With the abrupt switch from breastmilk to formula.

However after the fourth waking
I watched as he
Opened his big blue eyes
To stare up at me momentarily
Then with a soft whimper
He would look around frantically.
I realized,
He was searching
For you,
I'd hold him and our eyes would meet
And he would cry out again,
Even as I rocked him,
Because you weren't there
And he knew.
He would writhe in my arms,
He did not want milk or lullabies,
He only ever wanted you,
His mommy.
His heart would break at each waking,
Mine would break alongside his
I did what I could-
Swaddling, cuddling, rocking, humming, singing soft
lullabies, and cradling him in my arms.
My own tears mixed with his
As I gently rubbed his back.
My heart heavier than my eyes,
I felt so helpless and heartbroken,

I could only think to say
"I am so sorry, sweet boy".
Eventually exhaustion took over and he fell asleep.
I carefully carried him back to the air mattress,
Placed him gently between my husband and I,
Ensuring he was surrounded with love and safety.
His tiny snores punctuated the too quiet
Of a home
Steeped in grief.

Two years later
My love for you is also my love for him.
Strong and ferocious.
I would lay down my life for his
In a heartbeat-
The way I wish I could have done for you.

You deserve to be here with him,
With all of us.

I see so much of you in him-
In his cheeky smile,
In his fiery personality,
His love for adventure.
You must be so very proud of him.

Please know this, Alyona,

I’ve got him-
I love him the way you loved my babies,
Unconditionally and without ulterior motives.
I won’t ever stop.

5. Reclaim

Tonight
I sang karaoke
For the first time
Since the last night
I was raped.

It was beautiful,
It was awful.

I cried in the bathroom
Before I went on stage.

I searched for a proud face,
I trembled,
Steadied my breathing
All while
My heart pounded like
A baseball bat cracking against a windshield.

But I did it.

Three minutes isn't very long
But tonight it felt an eternity.
Because every second
I remembered his hands on me,
His raspy voice,
Just everything.

But for three minutes
I stood my ground,
Let the screams become a melody,
Channeled all that hurt and grief
Into a shaky voice,
Into a cheap microphone
In a dive bar
Where are only a few people
Even knew my name.

I didn't stop thinking of him
In those three minutes
But I did take my voice back
At least for one night.
And for now,
That is enough.

6. Butterfly Effect

People frequently talk about regrets
And how they would do things differently
If only they could go back in time.

I don't know that I would though-
I have regrets
But every single choice I have made-
Good and bad-
Has led me here
To this moment,
To this beautiful life.

I have experienced so much
And with that experience comes wisdom-
It was hard-earned but it has illuminated so much.
I wish I had been gentler with myself
And even more so with those I love.
I wish I had been more open and
Truly appreciated the time I had
With people I have since lost.

But if I were to go back
And do even one thing differently
What life would I be living now?

7. Holy

I've never felt closer to God than
When I visited my great-grandmother as a child.
Early Sunday mornings were spent in a church pew,
My head in her lap, the cotton of her Sunday's best
pressed against my cheek,
Drifting to sleep to the sound of her singing along to the
hymns with the choir.
Holding her weathered King James bible,
In gentle, withered hands.

I don't remember the sermons from the preacher
But I do remember the sound of her carefully
Turning each page
And seeing her trace each passage, following along to
the preacher's voice.
Those humid southern mornings
Saturated with her warmth.

In those days,
Safety was a luxury I wasn't always afforded,

A resource that was scarce.
But when my mother dropped me off on my grandmother's doorstep
Hope and a sense of 'home' enveloped me
Just like her arms did.

Many afternoons were spent at the nearby BiLo,
Shopping for groceries-
She always made sure she had my favorite foods.
She would smile and laugh aloud
As I skipped down the aisles,
Collecting every single coupon from the dispensers throughout the stores-
We rarely ever used them but she still let me get every single one.
Then back to her house we'd go
Where she would cook
And lovingly allow me to 'help'-
Tiny dimpled hands mixing ingredients and setting the table-
Making more mess than anything else,
Except for maybe memories.
We'd bow our heads, fold our hands, and say grace at her kitchen table
Before every meal she painstakingly prepared.
Afterwards she would send me into the living room to play

While she cleaned.
I'd hear her humming in the next room,
And I would feel myself getting drowsy.
She'd gently scoop me into her arms,
Sit in her recliner and gently rock me to sleep.
When I woke up later
I would be tucked safely in her bed,
Cocooned in quilts that smelled like her.

I don't pretend to know much about God or saints
But I do know that *'Edna'* is synonymous with *'Holy'*.

8. Reflection

Art cannot always be beautiful

It comes from the rawest portions of life-
Shaped by experiences,
Molded by emotions.

Not everything is meant to be
Pretty or pleasing.
You cannot slap a bow on everything that
Life has dealt you.

Sometimes
It has to be ugly
And deformed-
Messy, chaotic-
A twisted broken thing.

Sometimes it has to make you
Ache.
Make you question everything,

Make you let out the most primitive scream,
And leave you in pieces.

Art imitates life-
And when have you ever known
A perfect life?

9. Harmony

I have always hated
Loud noises, bright lights
People crowding me.

It all becomes overwhelming-
Leaves me breathless,
Anxious and angry-
A ball of adrenaline.
Plotting exit strategies
Solely focused on the escape route,
So I can hide,
At least until the world feels
Just a bit 'less'.

But
Somehow a concert
Is entirely different,
Softer,
Safer.
The moment the percussion

Rattles my bones-
The sound waves pulsating through my frame
From the floor
To my feet-
Up, up, up.

I feel lighter somehow
Butterflies fluttering through my abdomen,
A quieting of my brain,
A blooming sensation
Spreading throughout my chest.

My head feels like it's swimming,
Floating,
Peaceful,
Tranquil.
Even as I feel the bodies around me
Everything is less abrasive-
A stranger's touch doesn't feel so scalding
Because we are all belting out the words
To the same songs
That saved us
Over and over again,
Once upon a time.

I think that **this**
Must be what camaraderie feels like-

The lights aren't so blinding
When they highlight the saviors
On stage,
Or when they illuminate
The kindred spirits
Surrounding me.

Every emotion raw and on your face-
Like looking in a mirror
On your best and worst days
Simultaneously.

It feels like being called home.

10. New Poem

Your heart must
Have been made for mine
With the way
You simply understand
How I collapse.

Drunk on your touch
Our ghosts danced magnificently
Together.

Kiss me until
Our bones begin
To sing.

Until our wounds
Have scarred over,
Leaving only the smallest
Indication of a life
Once so turbulent.

11. The Gardener

Only he can make
Poetry
In the depths
Of my soul.

He planted seeds
In the wreckage.
Diligently and lovingly,
He sowed
And nurtured.
Tending to the ruins,
Where life made a graveyard of my heart.

Patiently waiting
Until
Finally,
I bloomed

12. The Artist

When everything in this life
Feels like it is spiraling
Out of control,
When I feel the weight of
Helplessness
Suffocating me,
A boulder on my chest-
I **create.**

I bake bread,
Make pasta from scratch,
Nourishing the bodies of those I love.

I write,
Mixing my blood with ink,
Cleansing my soul.

I clean and organize-
My insides may feel tumultuous
But I can at least make my outside world a bit gentler.

I fire up the cricut, the heat press,
The 3D printer hums along
As I make something beautiful.

I put on music as loud I can bare
Drowning out the world as I begin to recalibrate myself,
Regulating the turmoil inside of me.

There are far too many things in this life that feel
inevitable-
Instead of resigning myself to that
I dig my heals in and do what I can.

13. The Author

He is
My Always.

Our love is
Breathing art.

This blooming
Between us

Will always be
My favorite chapter.

14. Everlasting

A vibrant hurt
Burns the same
As a broken promise.

My blood will leave
A bitter taste
In your mouth

For years to come.

15. Odyssey

Sweet poet,
Hungry artist,
Always mending.

I pray
Our sonnets
Live on
Long after we are gone.

Some poor souls
Never learn
How to create
Their own dawn.

16. Battle Cry

Moon child,
Gentle spirit.

Heavy sword
In quivering hands,

A horrid choice
Deep within your battered soul.

Say all that
Only you can.

They may never
Truly hear you.

But at least
You can say

Even with a trembling voice
You **fought** to be heard.

Be proud, my love.

17. Eons

Your spirit
Will echo
Through a million
Lifetimes-

And I will find you
In every single one.

18. The Architect

He is the storm
I didn't know
I needed-

He washed away
Aches and debris
From a war-torn past.

He helped topple
The crumbling remains
Of walls built by small hands.

Then he helped me
Lay a new foundation,
One I could build upon.

19. Foreign

The storm
Coursing beneath my skin,
Your loud love,
My apprehension
At odds
With one another.

You, fighting to show me
That love can be gentle,
It can be safe-
It doesn't have to
Consume everything around me
And leave me choking on the ash.

Me, operating only on survival,
Self-preservation.
I'd never felt seen or heard-
I had never truly been 'known'
By anyone;
And then you came along.

Your love-
It frightened me
Most days,
It still does at times.

How can anyone go from a
Never-ending Armageddon
To consecrated ground
Without waiting for
The other shoe to drop?

20. Valkyrie

Small
Strange
Body.

Delicate
Flesh.

Fragile
Smile.

Broken
Virtue.

The softest threat;

Remember how I spoke
Truth
With a sharpened tongue.

I will be your downfall.

21. Cataclysm

This life has a way
Of absolutely
And unequivocally
Throwing me loop after loop

I have loved,
Fiercely.

And I have lost,
Gut-wrenchingly.

So many things
Should have broken me,
But yet,
I am still here.

Some nights I spend
Replaying memories,
Wishing I had been
Stronger, smarter, **safer.**

But I was strong enough-
To endure,
To survive,
And later,
To **thrive-**

Despite so many roadblocks
Laid out before me.

Because all of this time-
I have been enough

And that changes **everything.**

www.ingramcontent.com/pod-product-compliance
Lightning Source LLC
Chambersburg PA
CBHW051744130826
49812CB00033B/989
9789370923782